100 Days
100 Drawings
Ocean Life

It's time to learn. It's time to practice.
It's time to improve yourself.

Austin Fabinski

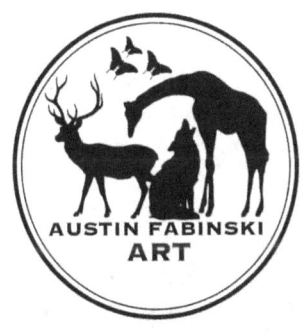

To learn and get better at something you must practice it. So what happens if you do a drawing everyday for 100 days? Take up this challenge and show yourself what you can do.

This book is filled with 100 Ocean life prompts for you to draw. You choose your medium and art style you want to do. Change it up or do the same for every prompt. The first 25 days starts with a minimum of 30 minutes, then time will be added every 25 days. You can challenge yourself to add the time, but at least stick to 30 minutes for each drawing. You do what you need to succeed in this challenge.

Let this book be your guide, inspiration, and motivation to help you improve your drawing skills and to make the habit to want to create something everyday.

Challenge yourself and have fun.

You got this!

Cover images credits: www.pixabay.com

100 Days 100 Drawings
By Austin Fabinski
© Copyright 2020 Austin Fabinski ART

Day 1 starts today!

RECOMMENDATIONS:
(PENCIL, COLOR PENCILS, CRAYONS, MARKERS, OR PENS)

REMEMBER TO HAVE FUN AND BE CREATIVE!

GOOD LUCK!

Day 1

Beluga Whale

(30 min)

Day 2

Sea Lion

(30 min)

Day 3

Marine Otter

(30 min)

Day 4

CORAL

(30 min)

Day 5

Eel

(30 min)

Day 6

Blue Crab

(30 min)

Day 7

BARNACLE

(30 min)

YOU DID IT! THE FIRST WEEK IS COMPLETED! WAY TO GO!

Day 8

Gray Whale

(30 min)

Day 9

Polar Bear

(30 min)

Day 10

Jellyfish

(30 min)

Day 11

OCEAN

(30 min)

Day 12

COD

(30 min)

Day 13

SQUID

(30 min)

Day 14

SHRIMP

(30 min)
2 WEEKS COMPLETED!
AWESOME WORK!

Day 15

Tuna

(30 min)

Day 16

OYSTER

(30 min)

Day 17

Bottlenose Dolphin

(30 min)

Day 18

Sea Sponge

(30 min)

Day 19

Blue Whale

(30 min)

Day 20

Walrus

(30 min)

Day 21

STARFISH

(30 min)

Day 22

CLAM

(30 min)

Day 23

Lobster

(30 min)

Day 24

NAUTILUS

(30 min)

Day 25

BEACH

(30 min)
You are doing amazing!
Keep it up!

Day 26

GROUPER

(1 Hour)
YOU CAN DO IT FOR LONGER!
I BELIEVE IN YOU!

Day 27

Cuttlefish

(1 Hour)

Day 28

SEAHORSE

(1 Hour)

Day 29

Queen Angelfish

(1 Hour)

Day 30

Saltwater Crocodile

(1 Hour)

You did it! You are making this into a habit! Keep it up!

Day 31

Pelican

(1 Hour)

Day 32

Orca

(1 Hour)

Day 33

Harp Seal

(1 Hour)

Day 34

Sea Urchin

(1 Hour)

Day 35

Caribbean Reef Octopus

(1 Hour)

Day 36

Light House

(1 Hour)

Day 37

Humpback Whale

(1 Hour)

Day 38

Blue Shark

(1 Hour)

Day 39

Spotted Eagle Ray

(1 Hour)

Day 40

Kelp

(1 Hour)

You have done this for 40 days!
Way to go!

Day 41

Queen Conch

(1 Hour)

Day 42

Leatherback Turtle

(1 Hour)

Day 43

Krill

(1 Hour)

Day 44

Hammerhead Shark

(1 Hour)

Day 45

Seagull

(1 Hour)

Day 46

Great Barracuda

(1 Hour)

Day 47

Seagrass Bed

(1 Hour)

Day 48

Atlantic Salmon

(1 Hour)

Day 49

Coral Reef

(1 Hour)

Day 50

Blue Marlin

(1 Hour)
Congrats!!!
Half way there!!!

Day 51

Ice Edge

(1.5 hours)
You can do this! Time management!

Day 52

Mahi-Mahi

(1.5 hours)

Day 53

MANATEE

(1.5 hours)

Day 54

Christmas Tree Worm

(1.5 hours)

Day 55

Hermit Crab

(1.5 hours)

Day 56

SEASHELL

(1.5 hours)

Day 57

Arctic Tern

(1.5 hours)

Day 58

Leopard Seal

(1.5 hours)

Day 59

MUSSEL

(1.5 hours)

Day 60

Loggerhead Turtle

(1.5 hours)

Can you believe it? You have done this for 60 days. Bravo!

Day 61

Atlantic Puffin

(1.5 hours)

Day 62

Marine Iguana

(1.5 hours)

Day 63

NARWHAL

(1.5 hours)

Day 64

Kelp Forest

(1.5 hours)

Day 65

Atlantic Trumpetfish

(1.5 hours)

Day 66

BLUE TANG

(1.5 hours)

Day 67

Clownfish

(1.5 hours)

Day 68

Leafy Seadragon

(1.5 hours)

Day 69

Parrotfish

(1.5 hours)

Day 70

Royal Penguin

(1.5 hours)

Day 71

Giant Manta Ray

(1.5 hours)

Day 72

Great White Shark

(1.5 hours)

Day 73

DUGONG

(1.5 hours)

Day 74

NUDIBRANCH

(1.5 hours)

Day 75

Sunken Ship

(1.5 hours)
Three-quarters completed!
Make sure you celebrate!!

Day 76

Sperm Whale

(2 Hours)

This is a challenge! The goal is to draw everyday. You got this! Break the time up.

Day 77

Blue Glaucus

(2 Hours)

Day 78

Sunken Treasure

(2 Hours)

Day 79

Dumbo Octopus

(2 Hours)

Day 80

King Crab

(2 Hours)

Day 81

Fugu

(2 Hours)

Day 82

WHALE SHARK

(2 Hours)

Day 83

Blue-Footed Booby

(2 Hours)

Day 84

SWORDFISH

(2 Hours)

Day 85

King Penguin

(2 Hours)

Day 86

Tiger Shark

(2 Hours)

Day 87

Collapsing Wave

(2 Hours)

Day 88

Hourglass Dolphin

(2 Hours)

Day 89

Giant Pacific Octopus

(2 Hours)

Day 90

Underwater Cave

(2 Hours)

Ten more days! You can do it!

Day 91

Elephant Seal

(2 Hours)

Day 92

Basking Shark

(2 Hours)

Day 93

Red Lionfish

(2 Hours)

Day 94

Deep Sea Anglerfish

(2 Hours)

Day 95

Coconut Octopus

(2 Hours)

Day 96

SEASCAPE

(2 Hours)

Day 97

Pacific Black Dragon

(2 Hours)

Day 98

Smalltooth Sawfish

(2 Hours)

Day 99

Two-Wing Flyingfish

(2 Hours)

Day 100

Your Favorite Ocean Life

(2 Hours)

Congratulations!
You did it!
Time to celebrate, reflect, and continue doing art!

What is next?

ANOTHER CHALLENGE?

Check out!

100 Days 100 Drawings

Dogs

Animals

Fantasy

---

100 Days 100 Drawings

Birds

Objects

Anatomy

Coming soon!

www.ingramcontent.com/pod-product-compliance
Lightning Source LLC
Chambersburg PA
CBHW080541220526
45466CB00010B/2996